AF413386

Masterpiece
in Your Heart

S. SULIANAH

Masterpiece in Your Heart

A SERIES OF POETRY

Second Edition ISBN: 978-981-11-6877-2
First Edition was published on June 2016

Poems by S. Sulianah
Edited by Kaitlin Severini
Arrangements and Concept by S. Sulianah
Cover Illustration by Vadha Hidayat
Cover and Interior Design by Euan Monaghan
Photographs by S. Sulianah

Photographs taken in New York, New York; Bettles, Anchorage, and Fairbanks, Alaska; Jungfraujoch, Switzerland; Paris, France; London, England; Hong Kong; Yakutsk, and Oymyakon, Russia; and Long Beach, California

I would like to dedicate this to the individuals who have
been part of my life, the inspiration for these poems.

Original Published Dates

Chemistry

The element of compounds
Us

$$C_8H_{11}NO_2 + C_{10}H_{12}N_2O + C_{43}H_{66}N_{12}O_{12}S_2$$

ESTP + ESFP

The amalgamation of your character and mine
The syncing of my thoughts and yours
The feelings we shared

Why, of hundreds of people
Are we the exceptions
Why you and me

Why our determination fits
Why our perspectives sync

That eye contact
How our gazes met

Those unmet contacts
Those magnetic actions

How our intelligence fits
When our counts are the same
Why us
And just us

The multiplication of our strengths and limitations
That subtraction of our strengths with our limitations

The opposite reflections of our likes
The square roots of our gestures

All fit well
Overwhelming

We as one

Perfect Everything

You always say that you lack this
And you lack that
Yet
You have the sweetest smiles
Genuine
Innocently addictive

You think that you are incapable of this
And you are incapable of that
Yet
You are talented
Determined and elegant

I remember
You were one of the smartest students in school
Beautiful
Charming

Your uniqueness

The comfort whenever I am with you
Thoughtful
Compassionate
Your adorable awkwardness

Your charisma
Is a charm to our relationship

You have been perfect
Always
Perfect with everything

Fading It

The feeling that fades
Temporary

The climax of thoughts and emotions
Overwhelming at the first instance

Weeks of exploring
Months of carving

In years
Neutralize to abstracts

The wonder of its authenticity
Its shadows
The truths of it all

PRIVATE EYES
GENTLEMEN'S CLUB

Our Ways

Whenever we listened to songs that are related to our life, they touched our hearts. How beautiful lyrics were formed naturally, reflecting our experiences and feelings.

Snippets of lyrics touched our life beautifully, leaving traces that magnified our memories.

That first time we were introduced
You had that calm aura
Neutral

I see you as that beautiful person
Who will entwine my heart
Again
If I do not distance myself

I managed to
Be away from you
Both

If I do not limit myself
This feeling will stay

This time I observed your elegance

I tried to minimize our conversations
Until you called me by my name
That melodic tone
Composed
Your signature of calmness

When I gave you the way
Instead
You opened up the door for me
That first time was not the only time

Last and recent
You touched my heart

We talked but not as much as with the others
It seemed like we communicated
Loud with silence

Our height differences
How tall you are
Stunning
Cracks open the little door to my heart

Your soothing eyes
Authentic smiles
Appeal with style

How we greet each other
Instead of handshakes
The hugs
The discreet touches

Unexpectedly
Your graciousness
Softens my pride

The distance and the energy
They become stronger than usual

How we are beside each other naturally
Since the photos two years ago
How our things are just beside one another naturally
Like one year ago

And now it is not just you
It is both of you

I heard you are smart
I see with my own eyes how smart you both are
That is one of the reasons
I have all these dreams about us

We can, without anyone knowing
Explore the world together
Hide our glances from others
Can we

It has been a while
Six months
We met each other
One another

You are still in me
Every flash
At times both of you
Do you

That moment
Captivated by you
Your touch
Your smile

Mainstream

Life
A natural flow
Calm

Our mindset is like the properties of the riverbed
A treasure to crystallize
The path
Beautify with purpose

Our goals are like the mountain ahead of us
Our determination helps us to never give up

The challenges
A bolster

Our self-assurance clasps our core purposes
Solidifies our integrity
Failures net our learned experiences

Bury away any external negativities
Boost our interests and motivations
An icing to our mainstream purpose

ICC
M

Epilogue of Hope

I like the way you skidded your car to stop me
I like the way you buzzed your car when you saw me
I have been longing to meet you again
Even though my heart whispers, "Please, don't . . ."

Your sudden appearance
For weeks of lullaby to your absence
Your presence is my distraction

You are definitely an impossible
We are an impossible

I love how all these moments with you had evolved
From ignoring my presence
To how we are now

Your smiles
Your humor
Your pleasantness
Your warmth
Your wit

The good news
I could not hide my shade of dim
The shadows of uncertainty
The gloom of my smiles

Mountains of walls begin to fence up
Again
Enveloping my thoughts
Shackling my epilogue of hope

The freezing breeze
Blanketing Anchorage Alaska

Mount Spurr is clouded by your presence

You look like that person
From four years ago
I could not take my eyes off your hair
Your eyes
Your cheekbones

When your hair drops, it reminds me of those shiny curls

Your eyes avoiding my glance reminds me of how I did that
To that person
Four years ago

Observing you through that reflection
Crystallizing the frames of art
Composed while you serve the patrons

I can feel the intense vibes
Maybe you sense it

You two are the look-alikes

Your Look-Alike

57
57
57
57
EXIT

Imaginations

Imagination
A phenomenal experience
To move
And drift
Away from our reality

Grasping it
Achieving it
The truth in ironies
Is a dream
A dream come true

Imaginations
Wild with focus
You might wonder
Its possibilities
Its true colors in reality

That someone
That empire
That feeling
You wonder

Fulfilling each and every dream
An encouragement
Live this life with
Paints of luminous blushes
Trying to understand
Its multifaceted abstracts

Living without imaginations
Is darkness
Dim of shiny crystals
And the dusk blue sky

Chirp My Name

Tuneful
Melodic
Isn't it
When someone special
Calls out your name

Pleasingly mild
Soft, choral
Chirping like the birds at dawn
As tranquil as the Lena river in winter
Rustling with harmony like the leaves in autumn

Beautiful
Calm
A heartiest warmth

That gush of feels
Those subtle lullabies
Sweet and gentle

Wonderland of Imaginations

That moment when you smiled
Inches away from me
Flashing your beautiful crystal-clear eyes
With that confidence
Intimidating me
Speechless

Meeting new people with confidence
That is my forte
But with you
It was different

Your sparkling eyes
I wondered what color they were
Pretty, comely green
Mysterious gray

Awestruck by your presence at that mezzanine
Walking towards us with grace
My heart mildly lingered to a beat

When you started to speak to me
Instead of the others
I knew that was the flinch to my worries

The walls that I built
They were not as strong as I'd thought

I built my confidence
Within those minutes of opportunity
Exchanging curiosity
With
Where you are from
What you are doing here

I noticed that you glanced at me
I took that chance to eliminate my intimidation
Towards you

Fifteen minutes
We talked
I suggested we take pictures
As I did not want you to slip out from my mind
And this from your mind

I feel your hand around me
Your head rests on mine
Your beautiful curly hair sending shivers up my skin
Your touch sneaks through my soul

Moments of that
Still clear in my mind

When I reached for you
A year later
You were gone

It's taken months to years
From just those few minutes
Traces of your presence
Your smile
Overwhelm my heartbeat

That December
We were meant to meet once
And then never

Though the urge to meet you
Brought me to the places of
my dreams
I will never regret

When I reached for you again
You were . . . gone

You knew nothing about this
That is all on me

I knew from the beginning
Avoidance has been the appropriate move
Recklessly
I let your presence illuminate
my senses

Imagining
The wonderlands of imaginations
Beautiful
Yet, not possible

Hi . . . Good Night

Hi
Good Night

Hi
Good Night

Anticipating the next time we meet again
What I could do with that graciousness of yours

Or will this just be another moment
To be scripted
A poem of non-attainable love
Out of the line

Grasping Ice-Cold Air

Expressing this discreet feeling
Finally
Though not to you

Without an instant doubt

Is like lifting a burden
Bearing it for four years
Grasping the ice-cold air

Those struggles
To avoid you
To overcome it
To rid you out of my mind
Without success

I feel this
Deep in me
Deep in my thoughts
Deep in my senses

It is still there

Seeing you
With that elegance
With those eyes
With that smile
Makes it all challenging

You have won this game
I could not fake it
I could not get rid of it
Just yet

You ... Are The One

Exploring You is the start of everything
I had not much interest initially
With my rebellions
Yet after years of those experiences
You showed me how life works

Life filled with the most challenging hurdles
I could not understand
I could not stand

The people
Amicable and amiable ones
Good-looking and charming ones
Hypocrites and the genuine ones
Thoughtful and the selfish ones

The goals
Effortless and demanding ones
Short-term and the long-lasting ones

Since the early years
Teens
Teens to adulthood
Adulthood

Every hope and dream
You made it come true
Every slight thought, you made me feel it
Every wonder and want
You made me realize it

I remembered asking You for myself
To excel for my exams

You gave it to me

I remembered requesting from You
To be the top three students in school

You gave it to me

I remembered asking from You
To thrive in my studies

You gave it to me

I remembered all those moments
The achievements in my studies
The strengths
To encounter the unpleasant challenges
And people

The courage and motivations
Whenever I felt like giving up
At all times

My dreams fulfilled

Education, experiences, finances, time
People who suit my character
Self-confidence with your will
Strong-willed and determined
My efforts became reality

You never asked anything in return

With
Prayers
Positive morals
Charity
Positive attitude

Every time I wanted to try something
That I desired
Mainly not the right path
You allowed me to go through the first stage
However, you halted every possible moment
That could lead me to be lost in pleasure

I could feel the numbness of the situation

I knew why
And I would not question you
Pondering it made me realize
All the wrongs in it
And that was not what I actually wanted

You are the one who understands
And listens
To every single expression of my soul
My thoughts
And my frustrations

No one or I should question you

With years of experiencing the challenges
You are the only One beside me
You are the only One who meets me with another person or situation
To make me realize and overcome every unpleasant moment

Every detail of my genuine wants and needs, you had it fulfilled
You are the only One who understands and could adapt to me

I look forward that if I ever leave this life
I will be in a positive and pure state
The way you love it
The way you expect from your creations
The way it should be for all of us

Anatomy

I want to talk to you more than anyone else in this room
Listen to you laugh
Your intelligent comments
Careful with diplomacy

My mind works in sync with my heart
And my whole body will want to be part of the same

Touching your hands randomly while we chat
Intertwine our fingers without any reason
Hidden from others, under the table or behind benches
While we still talk about everything and nothing

"I did not plan all this" would be a lie
As I am certainly aware and conscious
My mind harmonizes perfectly with my heart

All from the shines of yours
The starlight of genuinity
Being there at all times

Autumn & Us

You appear in my mind whenever I close my eyes
Imagining you and everything about you
Is like how I imagine autumn

The colorful leaves
Crisp, crystal maroon and bronze
Swiftly falling to the ground

I can feel your presence
As comforting as the scent of autumn

Whenever I close my eyes, I imagine moments with you
How you feel in my arms
How your smile brightens my mornings and days
How my heart beats nervously every time you lean on me

I imagine the first time I met you
Those enchanting eyes
Clouded by a tint of concern
The touch on my wrist
That moment you uttered "I am not sure if this right"

Those moments

You had taken everything
The nucleus of me

These are flashlights to my imaginations
Like colors of autumn subtly seeping through
The mysterious wonders ahead of us

Dreams that we strive to achieve together
Encouraging each other to accomplish vibrant chapters in our lives

Your determination intensifies my motivation
Your intelligence encourages me to embrace mine
Your elegance lights the dusk
Your charisma melts my rile
Your sweet tender affection is the soul

There are impossibilities
Yet you believe there is always a way
That you and I will seek that peak
Where colors of autumn shimmer in our hearts, filled of each other

With you by my side
I will always be yours
Your presence will make me smile
Soothe my nerves
As calm as the autumn breeze

One day
You
Us
In Autumn

A Decade of You

A decade
It has been more than a decade
Seems there are still layers of you in me
Though I had tried to peel off every minute of them

Every time someone mentions your name
I am speechless
Makes me smile

Every time I see pictures of you
My heart beats with no sense of rhythm

We never had been serious with this
Not official
Yet it seems you are the only one
I had my heart strings on
Till this very moment

When I heard about your parents
It was heartbreaking
I could not hold myself
I then understood

A decade

I could not stand your tonality
Your sarcasm
Those unpleasant words
That you imparted to our friends

In spite of these
I was never treated the same
Like you treated them

Pleased

Your stutters
Your enthusiasm
Your intelligence
Your dreams
Your hopes
Your eagerness
Your efforts in your interests

Your smile
That smile I knew
It was always different for me

Your support and excitement
When I had the highest scores on my math test
Your smiles whenever our eyes met
Those times you glanced at me when you passed by my class

Our exchanges of hi every time we were outside the teachers' office
The handshakes and wishes when we were the top students in our school
Those glorious moments

Then
The distance
I do not know what it was exactly

Me and my dreams
Me and my ego
Me and my fear
Me and my what-ifs
Me and myself

I am not regretting that I said no
Yet I am still wondering what if I had said yes
Those possibilities that I could not imagine

I tried to untangle my heart for someone else
To get rid of all this and you
Over the years

I do not intend to turn back
To apologize
To say yes

I chose this way

Life, it says
One will meet
With those who deserve each other

The cross-process of an
achievement begins from that
specific thoughts, a motivation,
plans, do, and appreciate.

GRAPHOLISTIC INTERNATIONAL
GRAPHOLISTIC.COM

Vena Amoris

The gem on your finger
Might have stopped me from telling you
How I feel towards you
The thoughts that I have
Every time I am alone in the darkness
Of my nights and early mornings
The wants and needs that could fill
The screams of my breathlessness
And faint murmurs of my soul

A Masterpiece in Your Heart

Sometimes it is unexplainable
Complicated
To forget that one person
Or the scenes that film your initial moments

For a mere few minutes
That could liquefy your thoughts
Melt your heart
Melt your defense
Melt your ego

Nothing seems to work
To let it go away
You tried . . . Yet
It simply seems not possible

You focused on all the flaws of that person
To ease your intent
Yes . . . it is different
In a day or probably in seconds
Then
No . . . you accept all the flaws

You knew that was enough
You had tried at that initial glance
You knew if you had moved forward
That person would have been . . .
A masterpiece in your heart

And true enough
Swayed . . . That person appeared
That captivating tint of gray in those brown eyes
Curls
Those subtle touches
Strange, foreign expressions
And that enchanting smile

That is all it takes
To make you forever
Be that person
Again
Yearning for that person's attention
With no chance of anything
That dream that you fear . . . happened

And you will never, ever be with that person
That distance you sacrifice
A puzzle to this masterpiece

Those Times Untold

The first time I met you
I avoided looking into your eyes

Unexpectedly
Part of my heart was hooked

The second time
I consciously told myself not to again
Avoiding the attraction you emitted
Avoiding myself through this same old thing
Repeatedly
That will end up in disappointment

This time
We had the ample time
To talk
Share

I swiftly opened the door for you
But, you insisted I go ahead
During that time
I simply thought it was nothing

This moment
I am so glad you did that
As I felt the only exception
Though that gesture might be normal for you
Your look of hope . . . probably
That I should join in the dinner
And that unexpected touch of your hand with mine
Before we parted ways

The third time we met
I was looking forward to it

I did not expect that I would have the chance to sit beside you
Let alone chat
And be your partner

I accepted the cake you offered
Though I was not really into it

You offered the door
You made me felt different that day
Just you talking to me

Your smile and the way you speak
Brightens my night

That special day
I remembered how flushed I felt
Hopefully . . . not that blatant

That unexpected hug made my night

As of recent
I could not stop myself
From looking at the photos of us
Taken candidly
Molding comfortably

Us, spaces away from the others
At every scenes

That short glance between us
Was overwhelming
That I will never understand

Those times and moments
You seem to be closer to me
You and that person
In many instances

Just you and me
Just three of us

Seems intentional
Or probably just my usual imagination

His and your intelligence are a charm

The last time we met
You were as appealing as you ever were
That final touch
Strong and natural
Brightens my day

I know once again
It will just be this
This untold and unspoken attraction
That will last as it is

Abstracts

A glance of you feels like a touch of breeze
Acknowledging it triggers my wandering mind

Yet I am still confused
With the abstracts of the intangibles

Those seconds and minutes beat
Painted with neons
Yet dim

Friends . . . Unveiled

Sailing in a life full of challenges
Stumbling upon the journey to success and happiness
Overpowering limitations and failures
Chance upon strangers

Strangers who become your friends
Friends who captivate your heart
Without you anticipating
They grounded you
When you are on the verge of believing
The meaningless of the bond . . . friendship

That friend who had revealed your inner selves
Your hidden personality

A friend who you met six years ago
In college

Who you did not anticipate
Unveiled your inner competitiveness
Helped you to overcome your limitations
As swiftly as the winter breeze
Her forte
Magnifying your interest in scripting . . . your hidden dreams

You learned the sense to compliment
As you were not brought up to do so

She . . . who was the first person to be there with you
Attempt unfamiliar experiences
Bring you to places
Lead you to places you thought you would dislike
She made a difference
By merely being your companion
The one who made you smile
Like the sunshine enveloping the miles
She was that friend you will always remember
The one who had unveiled your inclinations
Your hidden personality

Avoiding them is like muting the melody of your favorite song
For all time chirping in your dreams
They warm your heart and journey with love
Melting your doubts as crisp as the summer bliss

A friend who is neither your colleague nor anybody
You met her seven years ago

Fond of her was not in your imagination
Her neutral grace blended the way you think and react
Fearlessly expressing feelings
She showed you that reacting to what you feel is beautiful
If you feel affection for someone
Or love someone

Vividly expressing that is . . . picturesque
She, who could be mysterious at times
Could be one of them in this journey of yours
Who wholeheartedly expresses her loves

Tearing down the wall of defense you built years ago
The magnetizing glow of touches, kisses, and hugs
For any reason . . . She is that friend you refuse to bid good-bye
The one who had unveiled your inclinations
Your hidden personality

Determination is one of the
strategies to achieve your goals.
It is a belief embeds in you
When you fall
It finds its way
Your passion
For you to attain it

GRAPHOLISTIC INTERNATIONAL
GRAPHOLISTIC.COM

That Moment

That moment
When you wonder what this is all about
You think it is as it has always been
Probably it is not
You are just wondering what is this
And at that moment
You know that it is what it is meant to be

It might not be what you have been thinking
It is time to move on
When there is nothing much possible
Sometimes that journey
Is the explanation to your uncertainty
Your uncertainty and hesitation

Tomorrow

It will sure be yours

Tomorrow
Nothing much you think could not be done
Definitely there is

Tomorrow
If you think it will not be yours
One day it will

Tomorrow
Thinking about it
Motivates you today
So be it

Tomorrow
If it never comes
There will be another
Tomorrow

Tomorrow
There is no response
Be it
Move ahead
There is another tomorrow

Finally
Probably
You depict the illustration of its portrait

Growing Like a Seed

Standing in the middle of this vacant road
Imagining my life without these

These surroundings
The clattering of the bits and pieces
The clicks of movements
Of these strangers

Screeching of the windows
Chattering of the neighbors
Hidden behind those walls

The click and clacks of heels
From that stranger
Who just bypassed me

All these
Will not be felt
Without the breath
That He gives me

Me
Growing like a seed
On this arena . . . this land
This sphere

Shades of Platinum

Fading platinum
Streaks of #8B008B

Lit up from the scorching sky
Shadowing the lush greens
And careless touches of our digits

Cheat Code

The variance of our relationship
Distinctive from the others
The formula to solve these parallels

Trying to understand this bond we share
The jokes of our friends' clashing with our laughter
Under the lit-up RGB (139,0,139) Arco
Threading with care with all the questions

Stealing glances at each other across the corners
Coincidently sitting next to each other in occasions
Your smirks eventually make me shiver in silence
My vision spry with #C0C0C0 #FFFFFF

<p>

The way you talk about your likes
Is the <body> of my days to come
Our fingers brushing in need and innocence
At every chance we have
Have always been the <header> to my days

<p>

All these coincidences
And correlations

Is there any code I could embed all these as my daily dose
Formulas that could connect the confusions in this friendship
The   of hollow in our life that would have been filled with us together
If I knew the code to cheat my way to your <p> ♥</p>
This time, would I have the courage to invite you to be part of my dreams

About The Author

S. Sulianah explores the metaphors and ironies of the moments she experiences and expresses them in short stories, poems, and novels, carving the essence of life in motivational articles and phrases.

She believes that to achieve a dream, barriers are the interesting challenges to overcome. Looking back after achieving something is a way to be more grateful and appreciative.